BIOGRAPHY FROM
ANCIENT CIVILIZATIONS
LEGENDS, FOLKLORE, AND STORIES OF ANCIENT WORLDS

The Life and Times of

CHARLEMAGNE

Mitchell Lane
PUBLISHERS

P.O. Box 196
Hockessin, Delaware 19707
www.mitchelllane.com

Titles
in the Series

The Life and Times of:

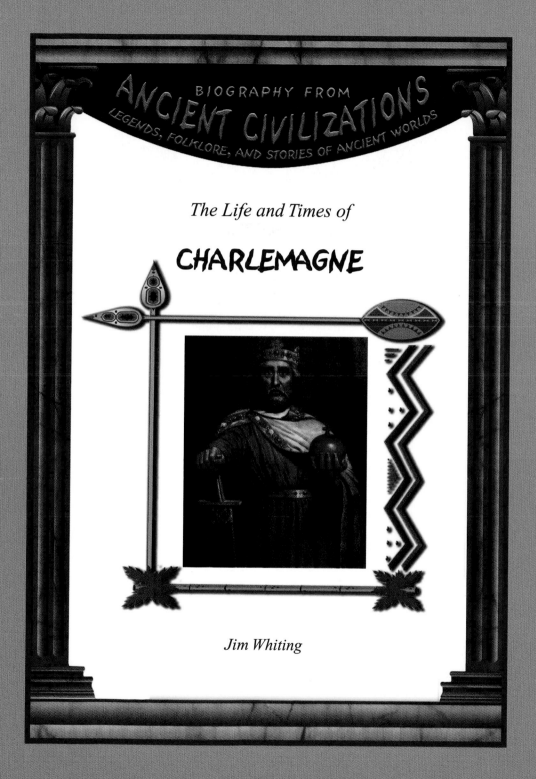

BIOGRAPHY FROM
ANCIENT CIVILIZATIONS
LEGENDS, FOLKLORE, AND STORIES OF ANCIENT WORLDS

The Life and Times of

CHARLEMAGNE

Jim Whiting

Printing   1   2   3   4   5   6   7   8
Library of Congress Cataloging-in-Publication Data

Whiting, Jim.
    The life and times of Charlemagne / by Jim Whiting.
        p. cm. — (Biography from ancient civilizations)
    Includes bibliographical references and index.
    ISBN 1-58415-346-6 (library bound)
    1. Charlemagne, Emperor, 742-814—Juvenile literature 2. Holy Roman Empire—Kings and rulers—Biography—Juvenile literature. 3. France—History—To 987—Juvenile literature. 4. Civilization, Medieval—Juvenile literature. 5. Southwest, New—Discovery and exploration—Spanish—Juvenile literature. I. Title. II. Series.
DC73.W47 2005

944'.0142'092—dc22

                                                                    2004024414

ABOUT THE AUTHOR: Jim Whiting has been a journalist, writer, editor, and photographer for more than 20 years. In addition to a lengthy stint as publisher of *Northwest Runner* magazine, Mr. Whiting has contributed articles to the *Seattle Times*, *Conde Nast Traveler*, *Newsday*, and *Saturday Evening Post*. He has written and edited more than 160 Mitchell Lane titles, including *The Life and Times of Julius Caesar* and *The Life and Times of Gilbert and Sullivan*. A self-proclaimed history buff, he lives in Washington state with his wife and two teenage sons.

PHOTO CREDITS: Cover, pp. 1, 3 — Getty Images; p. 6 — Andrea Pickens; p. 13 — Getty Images; p. 16 — Andrea Pickens; p. 22 — Getty Images; p. 30 — Library of Congress; pp. 36, 39 Getty Images.

PUBLISHER'S NOTE: This story is based on the author's extensive research, which he believes to be accurate. Documentation of such research is contained on page 46-47.

The internet sites referenced herein were active as of the publication date. Due to the fleeting nature of some web sites, we cannot guarantee they will all be active when you are reading this book.

The Life and Times of

CHARLEMAGNE

*For Your Information

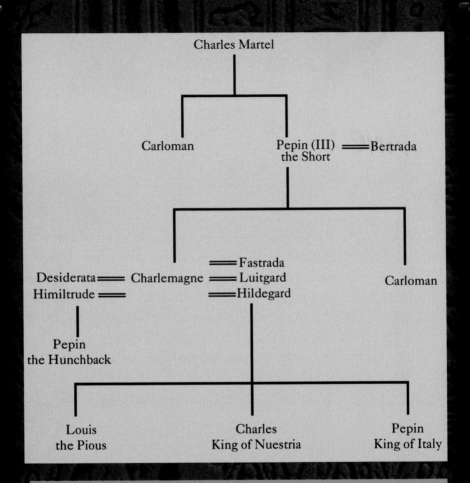

Charles Martel

Carloman   Pepin (III) ══Bertrada
                  the Short

                        ══ Fastrada
Desiderata══ Charlemagne ══ Luitgard   Carloman
Himiltrude ══   ══ Hildegard

Pepin
the Hunchback

Louis   Charles   Pepin
the Pious   King of Nuestria   King of Italy

This is Charlemagne's family tree. He was named
after his grandfather, who became a military hero
after a victory over the invading Muslims.
Charlemagne was an even greater warrior than his
grandfather. He also emphasized the importance of
education.

CHAPTER
ONE

LIVING UP TO A FAMOUS NAME

Sometimes young people overcome the pressure of having a famous name and become famous themselves. Race car driver Dale Earnhardt, Jr. won many of the biggest titles in the sport after his father died in the last lap of the Daytona 500 in 2001. Liv Tyler, the daughter of Steven Tyler of the classic rock band Aerosmith, was one of the featured actors in *The Lord of the Rings*. John F. Kennedy, Jr. spent his entire life in the public eye because his father had been one of this country's most popular presidents. He became a successful magazine publisher and appeared destined to accomplish much more. Unfortunately, he died in a plane crash in 1999.

Sometimes they don't overcome that pressure. In the year 475, Romulus Augustulus became the ruler of the Roman Empire. He bore two of the greatest names in Roman history. Romulus had been the legendary founder of the mighty city of Rome. Augustus had been the empire's greatest leader, so revered that the Romans changed the name of the month of Sextilis to August to honor him.

But Romulus Augustulus didn't live up to the expectations of his great names. It would have been a miracle if he had. For one thing, he was still a teenager when he became emperor. By that time, the empire had been split in half. The capital of the eastern half was at Constantinople (present-day Istanbul, Turkey). With a strong economic base and a strong government, what soon became known as the Byzantine Empire was doing well.

The western half, Romulus Augustulus's share of the empire, had been in a steady decline. The emperors had little actual power. Rome itself—which remained the capital—had even been captured twice, in 410 and 455, and many of its treasures had been carried off. The captors were so-called "barbarian" tribes, who roamed freely across lands once under the firm control of the Roman army. Conditions were so chaotic that hardly anyone noticed when a general named Odoacer overthrew Romulus Augustulus in 476. The boy was such a lightweight that Odoacer didn't even bother killing him. Instead, he sent Romulus Augustulus to a villa not far away, where the deposed ruler enjoyed a long and enjoyable "retirement" before dying of natural causes. It was only much later that people realized that Romulus Augustulus had been the last of the Roman emperors.

While the city of Rome remained important because it was the center of the Christian church, the rest of the western empire fragmented into a number of smaller kingdoms. When the Roman Empire had been strong, most people had lived in relative security. Now they lived in fear and uncertainty. As a Roman bishop who lived during this era noted, "See how swiftly death comes upon the world and how many peoples the violence of war has stricken. Some lay as food for the dogs; others were killed by the flames that licked their homes. In the villages and country houses, in the fields and in the countryside, on every road—death, sorrow, slaughter, fires, and lamentation."[1]

One of the kingdoms to emerge during this turbulent time was that of the Franks. A tribe that was originally from present-day

Germany, they migrated west and settled in what is today France (the name France comes from the name of the tribe). Under the leadership of a young king named Clovis, they significantly enlarged their territory. Perhaps even more important, Clovis became a Christian. So did his followers.

After Clovis died in 511, Frankish kings became less and less important. The real power was invested in noblemen who were known as mayors of the palace.

As a contemporary writer sarcastically noted, "There was nothing left the for King to do but be content with his name, his flowing hair, and long beard. . . . When he had to go abroad, he used to ride in a cart, drawn by a yoke of oxen, driven, peasant-fashion, by a ploughman."[2]

The king may have had little to do, but two centuries after Clovis's death, the mayors of the palace had their hands full as they confronted a new threat. The warriors of Islam—the Muslims, or Moors, as they were also called—erupted out of the Arabian desert and surged across North Africa. In 711, they crossed into Spain. Soon they threatened the southern borders of Frankish territory.

In 732, the Muslims launched a major invasion. As writer John J. Butt notes, "This was a threat against the kingdom, but also a Muslim threat against Christianity that if unstopped might signal the end of Christianity in the West."[3] Moving through central France, they encountered a Frankish army commanded by Charles, the mayor of the palace, between the cities of Poitiers and Tours. Charles led his troops to a decisive victory and the Muslims went back to Spain. As a result, he became known as Charles Martel, or Charles the Hammer, because of his skill with that weapon as he "pounded" his enemies.

Charles died in 741. His son Pépin succeeded him as mayor of the palace. Pépin decided to go one step further. Since he was king in fact, he would also be king in name. Without any difficulty, he deposed Childeric III, the king, in 751. To make his crown more legitimate, he asked the Pope to support him. The Pope sent a representative, who brought holy oil to anoint Pépin. Nearly 200 years after the time of Clovis, the Franks were united again under a strong king—and a king who was associated with both the Christian church and the legacy of the Roman Empire.

By then, Pépin had a son. He named him Charles after Charles Martel, hoping the boy would grow up to be like his renowned grandfather. From a young age, Charles would have known about the heroic exploits of his namesake. He would have known that he had a famous name to live up to. This knowledge would have put him under a lot of pressure.

During the course of the next five decades, Charles would live up to his grandfather's name. In 800, he would be given another name: Augustus. He would also live up to that name, which had not been bestowed on a ruler since the unfortunate Romulus Augustulus more than three centuries earlier.

After his death, he would be given yet another name. This time it would be a name for other people to try to live up to. He became one of the very few people in world history to have the word "great" added to his or her name. In the version of Latin that he spoke, his name became Carolus Magnus. In English, Charles the Great. But he is most famous for the version in French, a language he never knew but which his accomplishments helped to bring about.

That name is Charlemagne.

The Rise of Islam

Muhammad

The religion of Islam was founded by Muhammad, who was born in the Arabian city of Mecca about A.D. 570. He belonged to one of the numerous tribes that lived in the area. His father died before he was born, and his mother and grandfather died soon afterward. He was raised by his other relatives. As an adult, he developed a reputation for being honest, and he married a wealthy widow. He became concerned that tribal values such as honesty and generosity were being supplanted by greed.

Muhammad liked to go by himself into the desert to pray. One day in 610, he had a vision of the angel Gabriel. Both his wife and a Christian friend assured him that his vision was real. He had many more visions in the coming months. During these visits, Gabriel told Muhammad that he had a duty to instruct people, especially about the importance of submitting to the will of God—or Allah, as he is known among Arabs. But when Muhammad began spreading the word of Allah, he was persecuted. In 622 he fled from Mecca to the desert town of Yathrib (today's Medina). This flight became known as the hegira, and the Muslim calendar is dated from this event.

Muhammad began preaching. At first, people memorized his words. Then they began writing them down in what became the holy book of Islam, the Qur'an, or Koran. Muhammad led an army against Mecca beginning in 624. By 630, the city submitted to the invaders. Two years later Muhammad died. Under the leadership of several caliphs, his successors, the desert tribes became united under the banner of Islam and quickly began expanding their territory. Muslim troops defeated much larger armies because they were expert horsemen, more mobile, and could easily live off the land.

Their religion was easy to understand and offered an attractive alternative to oppressive regimes such as the ones in Persia, Byzantium, and Egypt. Soon the Islamic empire became one of the largest in the world, stretching east from the Atlantic to the Indian Ocean.

This formal portrait of Charlemagne was probably made sometime around the year 800. His right hand supports a jeweled ceremonial sword. The globe he holds in his left hand symbolizes the earth. The cross at the top represents the Christian faith.

CHAPTER
TWO

ESTABLISHING A REPUTATION

Most historians believe that Charles was born in 742, probably on April 2, though there is little agreement on the location. He had one brother, Carloman, who was born nine years later. A sister, Gisela, probably was born about 758.

Several years after Charles's death, his friend and biographer Erhard wrote, "It would be folly, I think, to write a word concerning Charles' birth and infancy, or even his boyhood, for nothing has ever been written on the subject, and there is no one alive now who can give information on it."[1]

What little information we have suggests that from an early age Charles was raised to prepare him for the pressures of military campaigns and governing large groups of people. In that era, one of the important qualifications for governing was physical fitness. There seems to be no doubt that Charles was a prime physical specimen. He would have needed to be to swing the heavy swords that were the characteristic armament of Frankish warriors. Even among that group, however, Charles stood out. When his grave was examined long after his death, it was found that he stood well over six feet, as much as a foot taller than the majority of the men whom he led into battle. Given this impressive stature, in all likelihood Charles was probably always "big for his age."

Since Charles was such a big man, it is curious that his father's nickname was "Pépin le Bref," or Pépin the Short. It is possible that Charles's size may have come from Bertrada, his mother. Her nickname was "Berte au Grand Pied," or Bertrada of the Big Foot, which suggests that she was a tall woman. She was also called Queen Goosefoot. Some people believe that "Queen Goosefoot" was the origin of the name for the popular Mother Goose children's rhymes that were published nearly a millennium later, especially since Bertrada had a reputation for caring about children.

Perhaps Charles had some time for rhymes as he was growing up. In an age when hardly anyone—even the clergy—could read or write, his father wanted to make sure that his son was literate. He hired Fulrad, the abbot of the monastery of St.-Denis (a suburb of present-day Paris) to serve as his son's tutor. As a man of God, Fulrad would also have taught Charles the importance of the Christian religion. So did his mother, who was a very devout Christian.

The most momentous event during Charles's boyhood came shortly before his twelfth birthday. Pope Stephen III was concerned about the possibility that Rome could be captured by the Lombard kings, who controlled much of the Italian peninsula. The popes before Stephen had used their powers of persuasion to keep the Lombards from taking over the city. Stephen had been less successful. The Lombards were making serious threats against him. Even though he was an elderly man, Stephen made a desperate winter journey through the snow-covered Alps to meet with Pépin. The two men arrived at a mutual understanding. Pépin agreed to provide military support against the Lombards. The Pope personally crowned Pépin and his two sons as kings of the Franks. He decreed that the Franks had to choose their future kings from Pépin's family. He also gave Pépin the title of patricius Romanorum, or "protector of Rome."

The coronation would have been a memorable ceremony for a boy who wasn't even a teenager. It would have impressed him with the knowledge that at some point he would assume power—and share it with his brother. His father was aware of the heavy responsibilities that would eventually fall onto their shoulders.

Pépin made sure that his sons had ample opportunity to learn how to rule. As soon as Charles was old enough to understand what was going on, he watched his father administer justice. Later he fought in several battles. In 764, Pépin went even further. He made his sons the administrators of a group of several counties.

By then it must have been evident to Pépin that the two brothers didn't get along. Their rivalry had to be restrained while he was still alive. The gloves came off in 768, as soon as he died. He had divided the kingdom between the two of them. Charlemagne received Austrasia, Neustria and most of Aquitaine. Carloman's domains included Alemannia, Burgundy and eastern Aquitaine.

Probably testing the young ruler's strength, the province of Aquitaine—part of the territory given to Charles—revolted in 769. Charles asked his brother for support. Carloman refused. Militarily, it didn't matter. Charles quickly emerged victorious. In terms of their already poor relationship, it did matter. The horrors of a destructive civil war began to seem likely.

Like most mothers, Bertrada loved her sons. She hated to see them fighting each other. Not unreasonably, she tried to reconcile

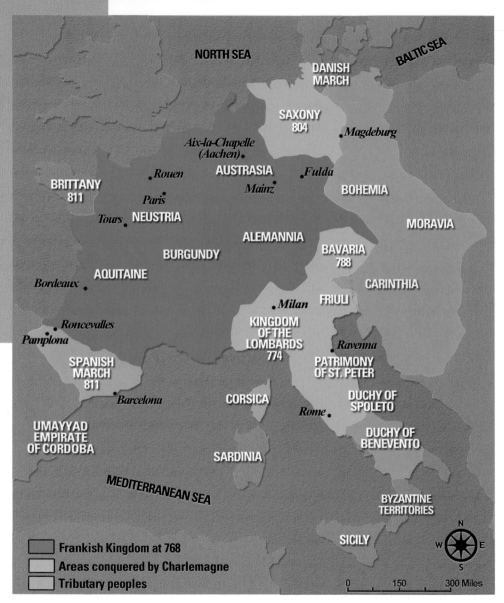

NORTH SEA

BALTIC SEA

DANISH
MARCH

SAXONY
804

Magdeburg

*Aix-la-Chapelle
(Aachen).*

Rouen AUSTRASIA *Fulda*

Mainz BOHEMIA

BRITTANY
811

Paris

Tours NEUSTRIA

MORAVIA

ALEMANNIA

BURGUNDY

BAVARIA
788

AQUITAINE

CARINTHIA

Bordeaux

Milan FRIULI

Roncevalles

Pamplona

KINGDOM
OF THE
LOMBARDS
774

Ravenna

SPANISH
MARCH
811

PATRIMONY
OF ST. PETER

Barcelona CORSICA

Rome

DUCHY OF
SPOLETO

UMAYYAD
EMIRATE
OF CORDOBA

DUCHY OF
BENEVENTO

SARDINIA

MEDITERRANEAN SEA

BYZANTINE
TERRITORIES

SICILY

N
W E
S

☐ Frankish Kingdom at 768
☐ Areas conquered by Charlemagne
☐ Tributary peoples

0   150   300 Miles

*This map shows the Frankish kingdom at the time of the death of Charlemagne's
father. Charlemagne received Austrasia, Neustria and most of Aquitaine.
Carloman's domains included Alemannia, Burgundy and eastern Aquitaine. The
map also shows the territory that Charlemagne eventually added.*

them. She thought that they should pursue a common policy, to try to be on good terms with both the Lombards and the Pope. One way of accomplishing this goal would be for Charles to marry Desiderata, the daughter of Desiderius, the Lombard king. The only problem was that Charles already had a wife. Named Himiltrude, she had given him a son, named Pépin after his grandfather. Charles's mother persuaded him to divorce Himiltrude—an easy step—and marry Desiderata.

In the meantime, Carloman had also married, and his wife Gerberga quickly gave him two sons. He chose to name his elder son Pépin, even though Charles's son had the same name. By choosing a name that Charles had already claimed for his son, Carloman was directly challenging his brother.

Soon there arose another source of competition. It became apparent that Bertrada's efforts to patch things up with the Lombards wasn't working. Charles had little interest in Desiderata. Being married to her didn't bring him closer to the Lombards. As patricius Romanorum, he supported the Pope. Carloman supported the Lombards.

Death solved the problem. Carloman died unexpectedly in 771. His widow didn't trust Charles with her life. She and her young sons headed for the court of the Lombards for protection.

Charles retaliated by sending Desiderata back home. He may have had another reason for rejecting her. Several sources suggest that she was physically weak, making it unlikely that she could bear the robust children that Charles expected. He didn't waste any time replacing her. He quickly married a girl named Hildegarde, who was probably only thirteen or fourteen at the time. Nor did he waste any time taking over his dead brother's lands, which provided him with many more men for his military campaigns. The campaign in Aquitaine in 769 had been his first. Fifty-two more would follow in his remaining years as king.

In spite of the mutual animosity between Charles and the Lombards—sending Desiderata back home was a serious insult—Charles's next campaign went in another direction. In 772, a band of Saxons, whose land was on the northeastern border of his kingdom, burned several churches in Frankish territory. The two sides had very little in common. One of the most important differences was religion. The Franks were Christians; the Saxons were pagans.

As Einhard comments, "No war ever undertaken by the Frank nation was carried on with such persistence and bitterness, or cost so much labor, because the Saxons, like almost all the tribes of Germany, were a fierce people, given to the worship of devils, and hostile to our religion, and did not consider it dishonorable to transgress and violate all law, human and divine. . . . [Charles] never allowed their faithless behavior to go unpunished, but either took the field against them in person, or sent his counts [noblemen] with an army to wreak vengeance and exact righteous satisfaction."[2]

Charles obtained satisfaction this time by leading a relatively small army into Saxon territory. His major accomplishment was pulling down the Irminsul, an elaborately carved tree that was a focal point for the Saxons when they worshiped their gods. The tree also contained substantial amounts of gold and silver. As soon as Charles finished this campaign against the Saxons, he began planning another and much larger one that would begin the following spring.

Before he could carry out his plan, he received a plea for help from the new pope, Adrian I. The Lombards were once again threatening to capture Rome. This was virtually the same situation that Pépin had confronted nearly two decades earlier. Pépin had intervened successfully, defeating the Lombards in several battles. When he withdrew, however, the Lombards never turned over to the Pope the lands they had promised they would. Charles's response was the same as his father's. He raised an army and marched against his former father-in-law.

He had another reason for urgency. Desiderius wasn't just trying to capture land. He hoped to "persuade" the Pope to declare that Pépin, the toddler son of the dead Carloman, was the true king of the Franks. With his own reign still in relative infancy, Charles could have been vulnerable to such a challenge.

Even though Charles's men were not experienced in the mountains, they easily crossed the Alps and captured several cities. At some point Charles gained control over Gerberga and her two baby sons. No one knows what happened to them, though the likelihood is that he sent them to a monastery rather than killing them. What is certain is that Charles continued on to Rome, where he received a triumphant reception and celebrated Easter.

Up to this point he had shown himself to be his father's worthy heir. Now he showed that he would go beyond what Pépin had done. He didn't want to have to deal with the Lombards again, so he had himself crowned as the Lombard king. It was his first step in expanding the lands of the Frankish kingdom. It would be far from his last.

He couldn't stay long in his new kingdom. He had been gone from his home for more than a year during the campaign. The Saxons had taken advantage of his lengthy absence to stir up trouble again. This time they were much more dangerous. Normally they fought in small bands, which was bad enough. Now they were united under the leadership of a chieftain named Widukind (sometimes spelled Wittekind). They were also outraged at the destruction of the Irminsul three years earlier. They began a campaign against Christian churches. Charles struck quickly and won several victories. Each time he won, he tried to force the conquered Saxons to convert to Christianity.

Charles had to take time out in the spring of 776 to return to Lombardy and defeat an attempt to overthrow his authority. He not only succeeded in that effort but was able to return to Saxony rapidly enough to suppress any renewed attacks. The following spring, he constructed a massive new fortress at Paderborn, a town inside Saxony. He named it Karlsburg, after the German form of his name, Karl. He conducted his annual assembly of Frankish nobles there. It was probably the first time that this important ceremony had been held outside actual Frankish lands. He invited the defeated Saxons to attend the assembly. Many were impressed enough by his military skill to accept his invitation to become Christians.

To his surprise, Charles received a visit from another group of men during the Paderborn assembly. They had no interest in becoming Christians. They wanted to take advantage of Charles's military muscle.

Charlemagne's Army

A Spear

The keys to Charlemagne's dozens of successful military campaigns were the men in his army and his ability to lead them. Charles was no stay-at-home king. While he rarely led his men personally in battle, his men knew that he was close by, directing the tactics that almost always spelled victory. They also knew that he cared for them, making sure that they were well fed and sheltered.

Every man in Charlemagne's army was responsible for furnishing his own equipment. Most had their own horses, but historians aren't sure how many actually rode their horses in battle. The ones who did wore helmets and padded leather jackets that contained some metal plates, and they carried small round shields. Their primary arms were heavy two-edged swords—considered the finest in Europe— and long lances. Infantrymen carried spears, short swords (nicknamed "flesh cutters" and "bone breakers"), bows and arrows, and shields. Few had any kind of body armor.

What makes Charles's victories especially remarkable is that he didn't have the benefit of a standing army. Every Frankish freeman was liable to be called up, though in any year only a fraction would actually be summoned. The men normally began assembling in the early spring and served for three to six months. Then they went home again, hopefully in time to help with the fall harvest. The short duration of service made it almost impossible to conduct training exercises.

Charles planned his campaigns months in advance, which was very unusual for that era. He went over every detail that he was likely to encounter. Once in the field, his favorite tactic was to split his troops into two divisions. Coupled with the fact that his forces had a reputation for moving much faster than was customary at that time, this split kept his opponents off-balance. They weren't sure where or when the two divisions would turn up. When the Franks were reunited, they would deliver a powerful attack that was almost always successful.

This painting depicts one of the many battles that Charles's army fought. His superior tactics almost always resulted in victory. These victories added a great deal of territory to the land that Charles inherited after the deaths of his father and brother.

CHAPTER
THREE

CREATING AN EMPIRE

During the Paderborn assembly, a group of Muslims traveled across France from Spain to meet the young Charles. Their leader, Suleiman Ibn Al-Arabi, was the ruler of Saragossa (present-day Zaragoza). Suleiman had led a revolt against the emir of Cordoba (who controlled a much larger portion of Muslim Spain) and wanted Charles's support. In exchange, he offered Charles the control of several cities near the Frankish border and the surrounding territory.

Suleiman's proposal was especially well timed because it showed Charles how far his fame had spread. Just over forty years before, the Muslims had been his grandfather's bitter enemies. Now some of them were humbly seeking his help. Besides the ego satisfaction, there were practical reasons for considering their offer.

It would add more land to his kingdom, helping to serve as a buffer against possible Muslim invasions. As long as they were still in Spain, the Muslims would represent a threat to Christians. While the Pyrenees Mountains in southern France were a formidable barrier, they were less of an obstacle close to the Mediterranean Sea. The land Suleiman was offering would help to seal off this potential access. Charles also believed that his fellow Christians were suffering greatly under Saracen, or Muslim, rule. Freeing them from this oppression would be a very good thing.

Soon after Easter the following year, Charles assembled the largest army he had put together thus far in his reign. Heading south, he crossed through the passes of the Pyrenees and halted at Pamplona (famous today because of the annual ceremony of the running of the bulls, in which hundreds of people risk serious injury or even death by dashing through the city's streets, where a herd of bulls has been released). There he received his first shock. Even though Christian Basques controlled the city, they resisted him. Charles had to capture the city by force, killing a number of the very people he was supposedly trying to rescue.

It seemed apparent that his understanding of the relationship between Spanish Christians and Saracens was not entirely correct. While some Christians were unhappy under Saracen rule, others were satisfied with the situation. Muslims were often more tolerant than Christians of other religions. One reason was that Islam, Judaism, and Christianity had a common root—the Old Testament of the Bible.

Charles's troops moved on to Saragossa, the main target of the campaign. But the situation had changed. Suleiman no longer controlled the city. In addition, the Muslim reinforcements that Suleiman had promised never showed up. Saragossa's defenders had no intention of surrendering, so Charles began a siege. He had provisions for only a few months in the intense Spanish summer heat. He soon had to discontinue the siege. On the way back, he destroyed much of Pamplona, further angering the Basques.

When the army reached the Pyrenees, with Charles at their head, most of the troops passed through the narrow mountain pass of Roncesvalles without incident. The rear guard lagged behind.

They were responsible for watching over the baggage train and protecting the main force. Without warning, they were attacked by Basques seeking revenge for the destruction of Pamplona. Though they were lightly armed, the attackers had the advantage. In the narrow pass, horses and heavy swords weren't very effective. The main body was so far ahead that they couldn't hear the rear guard's desperate cries for help. The carnage was complete. There were no survivors. The casualties included several important nobles, one of whom was Roland. When Charles returned, he wanted revenge, but it was impossible to follow the attackers into the heavy forests that surrounded the pass. Roncesvalles was probably Charles's worst defeat. An epic poem, called *The Song of Roland*, was written several centuries later. It honored the fallen Franks and would become one of the most famous literary works of the Middle Ages.

Adding to the bad news, Charles soon received word that the Saxons had—not surprisingly—decided to reject the oath of allegiance that had been forced on them. Widukind had returned to lead them, and Karlsburg had been burned. Already frustrated that he couldn't conquer the Muslims or the Basques, Charles couldn't immediately strike back at the Saxons either. The long campaign in the south had drained many men and resources. It would take time for him to rebuild.

Even the one piece of good news soon developed a downside. Hildegarde had presented him with twin boys, but one of the babies died. That was not a good omen. The surviving infant, named Louis (which honored Clovis, the first great Frankish king, giving the baby a name to live up to), joined two older brothers—Charles the Younger and Carloman—and two older sisters.

The following year Charles's army was strong enough to deal with the Saxons. After a series of Frankish victories, Widukind fled again. Charles felt confident enough to travel to Rome in 780. He had his three sons crowned as Frankish kings. He also had Carloman—his second son—re-baptized as Pépin. Charles wanted to keep that important name in the succession. The problem was that he already had a son named Pépin, by his first wife, Himiltrude. The solution was to declare the original Pépin illegitimate now that he had three other sons. For his purpose, it helped that the first boy was a hunchback, a deformity that made him seem unworthy among people who still retained a number of superstitions. Charles began formulating plans for dividing the kingdom among his three sons, even though he was still not forty himself and was in excellent health.

Thoughts of Saxony were probably far from his mind during these proceedings. Again Charles thought he had subdued the Saxons. Again he was wrong. In two years the Saxons would rise up again, prompting Charles to commit a crime that would blot his reputation. This crime would make it seem that he had returned to the barbarism that had once characterized the region.

The year 782 began innocently. Charles felt confident enough about the Saxon situation to hold the annual assembly in Saxon territory again. When it was over, almost everyone headed home. Charles heard that a band of Slavic invaders had attacked the far side of Saxony. Even though he believed the Saxons were capable of defending themselves, he nevertheless felt obligated to provide assistance. He ordered three of his most important nobles to lead a detachment of men to their aid.

It soon became apparent that Charles had been tricked. There were no Slavs. Instead there were thousands and thousands of angry Saxons gathered at Süntel mountain, led by Widukind, who had returned from his safe haven in Denmark.

Charles sent his trusted cousin Theodoric with more men to go to the aid of the original force, along with a careful plan. The Franks—the more mobile force with plenty of horses—would split and form a pincers movement that would catch the Saxon infantrymen between them. This was the same plan that had worked well on numerous other occasions.

Hearing of Theodoric's intervention, the three original commanders apparently became jealous. They wanted the glory for themselves. Instead of waiting for Theodoric, they made an immediate attack. They faced fully prepared troops who held the advantage of high ground, and nearly all of the Franks perished.

Charles quickly returned to the scene of the battle. Again he found the bodies of dead Franks. He felt the same outrage that he had four years earlier at Roncesvalles. This time he wasn't as helpless. He rounded up hundreds of Saxons at a town called Verden. He demanded to know who had led them. Widukind, came the reply. But Widukind had returned to his Danish sanctuary. Then Charles demanded that his prisoners give him the men who had fought with Widukind. About 4,500 men were brought to Charlemagne. He ordered them tied up and dragged into a nearby field, where they were all beheaded.

Einhard, wanting to preserve Charles's record as a glorious ruler, says nothing of Verden. Almost everyone else does. "The massacre shocked contemporaries," observes Friedrich Heer. "Many of his courtiers lamented that a ruler who had subdued whole kingdoms could not master his own brutal rage."[1]

A field full of corpses wasn't revenge enough. Charles issued the Capitulatio de partibus Saxoniae, a series of harsh laws directed at the Saxons. Death became the prescribed punishment for Saxons committing any of a wide variety of offenses, ranging from refusing Christian baptism to eating meat during Lent.

Not surprisingly, this harsh edict backfired. The Saxons arose again the following year. The renewed fighting wasn't Charles's only problem. Both his mother and his wife died within a few months of each other. Charles barely had time to mourn their loss. He was in the field continually. The Saxons couldn't stand up to him in open combat; they melted into the deep woods when he approached. After he passed, they would re-emerge and launch additional attacks against churches and other targets.

Sometime during the following year, Charles took another important step: he remarried. His new wife was named Fastrada, and she eventually proved to be as unpopular among the Franks as Hildegarde had been popular. In any event, Charles probably had little time to spend with her. He had taken the unusual step of keeping his army together through the entire winter of 784–85. Normally he let his men go home at the approach of cold weather.

The tactic paid off. Sometime in 785, Widukind offered peace. In exchange for surrendering and agreeing to be baptized, Charles allowed him to live. Finally the revolt began to fall apart.

With the Saxons apparently under control, Charles turned his attention elsewhere. The Lombards were stirring up trouble again. Charles led troops there to put down the rebellion. In 788 he defeated his kinsman, Tassilo III, the ruler of Bavaria. Now he ruled over nearly the entire territory occupied by the countries of present-day Western Europe: all or most of France, Germany, Belgium, The Netherlands, Switzerland, Luxembourg, Italy, Austria, the Czech Republic, and Hungary.

The Song of Roland

Roland sounding
his horn

For about three centuries, the annihilation of the rear guard and baggage train at Roncesvalles by angry Christian Basques was remembered only as one of the few defeats suffered by Charles. Then an unknown French poet composed *The Song of Roland.* It was a chanson de geste, or "song of heroic deeds," an important literary form that developed during the eleventh century. These chansons were performed by minstrels who wandered from town to town. They were very popular in an age when there were relatively few forms of entertainment.

Except for the presence of Charles and Roland, who are genuine historical figures, and the fact that all of rear guardsmen died in the battle, nothing else the poet describes in the long poem actually happened. It is a work of fiction that raised Roland from a battlefield casualty to virtually cult status. He became a legendary hero, a pure Christian warrior battling gloriously against a different—and hated—religion.

As the poem opens, Charles has conquered virtually all of Muslim Spain during seven years of fighting. Ganelon, a Muslim leader, decides to betray Roland as Charlemagne's victorious army begins its northward trek. A massive army of Muslims (rather than Basques) attacks the rear guard in Roncesvalles pass. Much of the poem depicts the heroic exploits of the twelve primary Frankish leaders during the battle. As they continue to fall in their fight against overwhelming odds, Roland's close friend Oliver urges him to sound an alarm on his huge horn. Roland refuses. He finally gives in to his friend's pleading when less than 100 men remain, but it is too late. Roland and Oliver exchange farewells and receive Christian blessing. Roland is the last Frank to die. The Muslims try to flee, but Charlemagne returns and defeats them. Then he executes the treacherous Ganelon by having him pulled apart by horses.

The Song of Roland firmly established its hero in European literature, where he became the subject of numerous other works in which he fought dragons and did other noble deeds.

This photo shows the cathedral at Aachen, Germany that Charlemagne built. It was the church of coronation for at least 30 German kings. Aachen Cathedral became a United Nations World Heritage Site in 1978.

CHAPTER
FOUR

THE CAROLINGIAN RENAISSANCE

Charles's reputation in history would be impressive enough if it were based solely on his accomplishments in battle and the resulting expansion of the territory of the Franks. But Charles's fame—and his future title of Great—lay on a broader foundation.

Because he had traveled so much at the head of his army, Charles was exposed to many other cultures in Europe. He was especially impressed by what he had seen in Lombardy. The region boasted some of the continent's best art and architecture. Its universities were centers of learning. He became aware that his empire would be even stronger if he could incorporate the best features of these other cultures.

The previous 150 years had been marked by barbarism. Charles's reign had appeared to move beyond this cruelty and backwardness—one reason that his massacre at Verden had been so shocking. For all his accomplishments in battle, Charles Martel had helped to accelerate this backward trend. In an effort to increase his power and unify the Franks, he had destroyed many centers of learning. Ignorance and illiteracy had become widespread throughout the Frankish realms.

His grandson would decisively change this dismal situation.

Charles recognized the value of literacy in administering a large kingdom. He became an advocate for education. Soon after returning from Lombardy the first time, he began a conscious effort to recruit the best scholars in Europe for his court, an effort similar to those used today by college coaches to recruit top athletes for their sports programs.

Charles also wanted to settle down. Following a long-established Frankish tradition, after becoming king, Charles had spent the vast majority of his time on the road.

As Butt observes, "In an era when laws and loyalty were only as good as the person who enforced them, a king had to show himself to reinforce his authority. As he traveled, the king would renew oaths of loyalty, enforce execution of laws that he had made and simply let everyone know that the king was present and could and would appear again if there was disobedience or disloyalty."[1]

The king's court—consisting of hundreds of people—usually accompanied him. Customarily, the king would travel from the villa of one nobleman to another. Feeding all those people for extended periods could present a major problem for even the most prosperous landowners. Charles's constant movement assured that none of the noblemen would have to bear this burden for an extended period of time.

Even for a man as vigorous as Charles, the continual moves became wearing. Around 790, his reign was sufficiently established that it was no longer necessary to always have to show himself to his subjects. Also, he was approaching fifty, just a few years away from the age at which his father and grandfather had died. He decided it was time to settle down and build his own capital—one that might rival Rome itself in its splendor. He chose the small town of Aachen (also known as Aix-la-Chappelle) in western Germany. For Charles, there was also a personal appeal. Aachen had warm mineral springs, which made it ideal for one of his favorite means of physical fitness: swimming.

The centerpiece was a large palace. One end was modeled after similar buildings built during the Roman Empire; the other end copied features of the Palatine Chapel. The chapel was a complicated building. It had sixteen sides surrounding an eight-sided inner temple, which contained many sacred relics given to Charlemagne from the popes.

Charles's ambitious building program made Aachen large enough and prestigious enough to serve as the focal point for what became known as the Carolingian Renaissance. The name Carolingian comes from Carolus, the Latin form of Charles's name, while renaissance is a rebirth or recovery of art and learning. Scholars from all over Europe began coming to Aachen. Many brought precious, irreplaceable ancient texts with them and probably saved them from destruction.

Charles became personally involved in this renaissance. As Einhard notes, "[Charles] most zealously cultivated the liberal arts, held those who taught them in great esteem, and conferred great honors upon them. He took lessons in grammar of the deacon Peter of Pisa, at that time an aged man. Another deacon, Albin of Britain, surnamed Alcuin, a man of Saxon extraction, who was the greatest scholar of the day, was his teacher in other branches of learning."[2]

His interests extended beyond academics. Charles was also responsible for improving the legal system and major public works projects such as bridges and palaces. "Above all," Einhard notes, "sacred edifices [buildings] were the object of his care throughout his whole kingdom; and whenever he found them falling to ruin from age, he commanded the priests and fathers who had charge of them, and made sure by commissioners that his instructions were obeyed."[3]

Charles couldn't devote all his energy to overseeing his cultural achievements. He still had to protect the borders of his empire, which involved even more fighting even though he wasn't especially interested in acquiring more territory. While his armies won most of these border conflicts relatively easily, that wasn't the case with the Avars. The Avars were descendents of the same tribe that had produced the notorious Attila the Hun several centuries earlier. They occupied land in central Europe. The border skirmishes turned to an all-out war that lasted several years. Finally Charles won the exhausting conflict, gaining some of the Avars' territory as a bonus. Another bonus was the Avars' vast treasury. Charles used the windfall to help finance the buildings at Aachen.

As time passed, Charles gained an additional advantage. His three sons became old enough to help him in his campaigns.

Another son, however, proved to be potentially dangerous. This was Pépin the Hunchback. While the date is uncertain—it may have been in the late 780s, while Charles was away campaigning, or even 792—a number of dissatisfied nobles convinced Pépin to turn against his father. According to Einhard, one of the main reasons for this dissatisfaction was their intense hatred of Fastrada. Charles learned of the plot and executed everyone except Pépin. Showing some unexpected softness, he allowed his son to live, though he banished him permanently to a monastery.

This plot would be the final challenge to his authority. Increasingly he began looking to the future. The immediate future, that is.

Then in 800, Charles made a trip to Rome. His footsteps would echo farther into the future than he could have imagined.

Alcuin

Alcuin

Probably the most famous figure in the Carolingian Renaissance was a man named Alcuin. He was born in York, England, around 735 and eventually became the headmaster of the school at York Cathedral. He also built up a large library connected with the cathedral, which attracted scholars from all over Europe. In 781, he was returning from a visit to Rome when he met Charles, who immediately recognized his ability. Charles invited him to join his royal court as director of the Palace School. It may have been a difficult decision. Alcuin—well into his forties—knew that he might never see his lifelong friends again.

On the other hand, he realized that he would have the opportunity to mold the minds of the empire's future leaders, especially Charles's children and the children of his most powerful nobles. Even more important, he would have the opportunity to mold the mind of Charles himself. Alcuin soon became a trusted adviser to the king. Many scholars believe that he was outraged at the massacre at Verden and encouraged Charles to become more merciful toward defeated enemies in future campaigns.

He was regarded as an inspiring teacher, who was especially interested in developing his students' ability to think for themselves. He was also an excellent administrator who helped to develop many other schools to further Charles's goal of education for as many people as possible. He was responsible for copying many ancient manuscripts, thus preserving them for future generations. He also wrote a great deal. His output included poetry and a number of letters that help to provide a picture of the living conditions during his era.

In 796 he moved to Tours, France, to become the abbot of a monastery. There he established a school and library. He died at the monastery in 804.

98

Pope Leo III was nearly killed by his enemies in 799 before Charlemagne came to his aid. After Leo crowned Charlemagne the following year, the two men worked closely together until Charlemagne's death. Leo died in 816, and was buried in St. Peter's Church in Rome. He became a saint of the Catholic Church in 1673.

CHAPTER
FIVE

THE EMPEROR

Five years before Charles's trip to Rome, Pope Adrian I had died. His replacement, Pope Leo III, had a number of enemies. In 799, these enemies brought serious charges against him. They physically assaulted him, trying to gouge out his eyes and cut off his tongue. Leo escaped and appealed to Charles for assistance.

Charles decided to go to Rome to make a full inquiry. His trip was delayed by the death of his queen Liutgard, who had become Charles's wife soon after the hated Fastrada had died in 794. He arrived in November and quickly cleared Leo of the charges. By then it was nearly Christmas. Leo had a gift for his benefactor. In a grandiose ceremony that echoed the glories of the Roman Empire, he placed a crown on Charles's head and solemnly said, "God grant life and victory to Charles the Augustus, crowned by God great and pacific Emperor of the Romans."[1]

It was a significant moment. It was the first time in more than 300 years that anyone had been given the title of Augustus. It was the first time that a "barbarian" had been king of Rome. And it was the first time that this crown had been bestowed by a pope.

That Christmas Day coronation was the high-water mark of Charles's reign. He spent the rest of his life consolidating his gains and preparing for his inevitable death.

One of his first tasks was to make peace with the Byzantine Empire. Since their territories included the island of Sicily and a small portion of Italy, there had been occasional conflict between the two sides. There was a deeper reason for discord.

The Byzantine Empire was the eastern half of the original Roman Empire. Its capital city of Constantinople had been founded by Constantine, one of the last important Roman emperors. The Byzantines looked at the Franks as the heirs of the barbarians who had destroyed the western half of the Roman Empire. Therefore, they regarded Charles's taking on the name of Augustus as an insult. They believed that the name belonged to them because they were the genuine heirs of the Romans.

More than a decade of strife followed Charles's coronation. Finally, a new emperor took power in Constantinople. He recognized the immense power that Charles had and finally recognized him as Emperor of the West.

Charles's new status as emperor didn't keep him from the battlefield. In 804—at the age of sixty-two—he led yet another campaign against the Saxons. It was their fourth uprising in twelve years. After defeating them, he forcibly resettled thousands of them in other parts of the empire—many as slaves—and gave their land to his fellow Franks. Thirty-two years and thousands of lives after the beginning of the conflict, it had finally come to an end.

Two years later he divided up the empire. Each son would be responsible for administering a substantial portion, with the title of emperor going to his eldest son, Charles. Remembering the awkward situation with his own brother Carloman, Charlemagne

This picture shows Louis, Charles's youngest son. Because his older brothers had died, he became emperor when his father died in 1814. Holding religious symbols in both hands symbolizes his deep Christian faith. He became known as Louis the Pious.

seems to have made sure that his three sons got along well. He had a great deal of confidence in his two older sons, considerably less in Louis.

"Of the three boys, Louis alone aroused [Charles's] misgivings for the future. He was a gentle little boy, deeply religious even as a child, fond of learning in a manner that could only win his father's approval, but also easily led and shrinking from the harsh world of battle,"[2] writes historian Russell Chamberlin.

Louis was little better as an administrator over the territories that he had been assigned. "Louis had proved totally incapable of imposing his will—so much so that his personal treasury was empty and he was unable even to buy the New Year presents which it was customary to exchange among relatives and close friends,"[3] Chamberlin continues.

Unfortunately, the two older sons died within a year of each other, Pépin in 810 and Charles the Younger in 1811. In 1813 Charles summoned Louis, made a last-ditch effort to prepare him for the responsibilities of administering the huge empire, then had him crowned emperor. He was just in time. A man who had experienced almost perfect health for virtually his entire life, Charles contracted a severe cold during the winter. The man who had won countless battles lost this one. He died on January 28, 814. He was buried in Aachen cathedral. His son—who became known in history as Louis the Pious—succeeded him.

Louis was unable to live up to the name he had been given, that of the great young king Clovis. At one point, his three sons even deposed him for several years. Though Louis regained power and died peacefully in 840, the empire he had inherited was already starting to fall apart. The following decades produced a complicated series of power struggles and land grabs involving Charles's descendents. Even though a number of them were named for him, none remotely approached "greatness," as indicated by some of their nicknames: Charles the Bald, Charles the Fat, Charles the Simple, and Charles the Child. His other less-than-outstanding heirs included Louis the Stammerer, Louis the Young, and Louis the Sluggard.

Some historians believe that the year 887 marked the end of the Carolingian empire. Charles the Fat was overthrown and replaced by a king who wasn't descended from Charlemagne. Others maintain that the end came in 962, with the formation of the Holy Roman Empire. Whatever the date, Jacques Boussard explains the result: "The widespread peace that the Empire had enjoyed under Charlemagne became a mere memory. All the western kingdoms were ravaged by continual wars. Not only did the ambitious rivalries of princes and nobles degenerate into conflicts and private wars, each laying waste his enemy's land so as to deprive him of means of support, but the frontiers were no longer safe from enemies outside the Empire."[4]

In the resulting chaos—somewhat similar to the conditions that had existed four centuries earlier with the collapse of the Western Roman Empire—Charles's reign took on a special status.

Just as Roland had passed from a historical figure to a legendary one after his death at Roncesvalles, something similar happened to Charles. His achievements, impressive as they were, were seen as a sort of golden age. He became an ideal ruler, a man who was a brilliant leader and brought out the best in his people by encouraging them to learn and to act morally.

More than eleven centuries after his death, this ideal was revived. In 1950, the city of Aachen established the Karlspreis (Charlemagne Prize), which has been awarded every year to individuals who have worked to bring about European unity.

FYI
For Your Info

The Holy Roman Empire

In 936, a king named Otto I— ironically, one of the Saxons, Charles's bitter opponents—had himself crowned at Aachen. Otto consciously viewed this act as continuing the empire that Charles had established. Yet he felt that he also needed the pope's blessing to fully become Charles's heir. That opportunity came in 962 when Pope John XII begged for Otto's support in overcoming a threat from an Italian king to invade Rome. In gratitude, the Pope crowned Otto as Roman Emperor. Many historians maintain that this event marked the beginning of the Holy Roman Empire, an important element in European politics for the next 800 years.

King Otto I (left) and his Queen (right)

In an important way, Otto's accession wasn't the same as Charles's had been. As a consequence of the almost continual fighting since Charles had died, the original Frankish kingdom was not a part of the Holy Roman Empire. By then, the Franks had split off and had begun their own succession of rulers. The two areas—one speaking French, the other mostly German—would develop in different directions. These differences would come to a head in the nineteenth and twentieth centuries, helping to produce the bloody horrors of World War I and World War II as French and German troops inflicted massive casualties on each other.

The Holy Roman Empire—the German-speaking portion—never enjoyed an emperor with the strength of Charles. Over the centuries, it slowly weakened before finally being dissolved in 1806. But its memory remained very powerful.

When Adolf Hitler came to power in Germany in 1933, he was eager to show that his rule was connected with his country's illustrious past. He announced he had established the Third Reich (from the German word for "empire") and boasted that it would last for a thousand years. The First Reich had been the Holy Roman Empire, while the Second Reich was the unified German empire that began in 1870 and lasted until the end of World War I in 1918. Fortunately, Hitler's prediction was in error. The Third Reich lasted just twelve years.

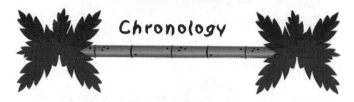

Chronology

742	Born on April 2
754	Given crown during visit of Pope Stephen III
764	Given responsibility to administer a group of counties
768	Assumes control of part of Frankish kingdom with death of his father, Pépin
769	Subdues a rebellion in Aquitaine; first son named Pépin is born
770	Marries Desiderata, daughter of king of Lombardy
771	With death of brother Carloman, becomes sole ruler of the Frankish kingdom
772	Sends Desiderata back to Lombardy; marries Hildegarde; begins campaigns against the Saxons; birth of son Charles (the Younger)
773	Attacks Lombards; travels to Rome
777	Birth of son Carloman (later renamed Pépin)
778	Leads expedition to Spain; rear guard under command of Roland is slaughtered during return; birth of son Louis
779	Attacks Saxons again
780	Travels to Rome, where his sons are crowned as his heirs
781	Invites Alcuin to become head of the Palace School
782	Executes 4,500 Saxons
783	Wife Hildegarde and mother Bertrada both die
784	Marries Fastrada
788	Takes over Bavaria
791	Begins building palace at Aachen to serve as his primary residence
794	Fastrada dies; marries Liutgard
800	Crowned Roman Emperor on Christmas Day by Pope Leo III; Liutgard dies
806	Divides kingdom among his three sons
810	Son Pépin dies
811	Son Charles dies
813	Gives power to his son Louis
814	Dies on January 28 in Aachen

Timeline
in History

A.D. 14	The Roman emperor Augustus dies after ruling for more than 40 years.
313	Roman emperor Constantine issues the Edict of Milan, which tolerates Christianity in the Roman Empire.
395	The Roman Empire is divided into two parts; Rome remains the capital of the West, and Byzantium becomes the capital of the East.
455	The Vandals, a barbarian tribe, sack Rome.
476	Romulus Augustulus, the final Roman emperor, is deposed by Odoacer.
570	Muhammad, the founder of Islam, is born.
622	The hegira—Muhammad's flight from Mecca to Medina—marks Year One in the calendar of Islam.
625	Muhammad begins dictating the Koran.
632	Muhammad dies.
687	Carolingians become hereditary mayors of the palace after Pépin the Younger wins the Battle of Testry to form the Frankish kingdom.
711	Muslims cross from North Africa and invade Spain.
732	Charles Martel defeats the Muslims in the Battle of Tours.
741	Charles Martel dies; Pépin the Short becomes mayor of the palace.
751	Pépin becomes king.
752	Stephen III becomes the Pope.
768	Pépin dies.
772	Adrian I becomes the Pope.
795	Adrian dies; Leo III becomes Pope.
814	Louis the Pious becomes king.
ca. 829	Einhard writes *The Life of Charlemagne*.
840	Louis the Pious dies.
962	The Holy Roman Empire is formed with the crowning of Otto I in Rome by Pope John XII.
ca. 1100	An anonymous French poet writes *The Song of Roland*.
1806	The Holy Roman Empire is officially dissolved.

Chapter Notes

Chapter 1   Living Up to a Famous Name
  1. Stephen G. Hyslop and Brian Pohanka, *Time Frame AD 200–600: Empires Besieged* (Alexandria, Virginia: Time-Life Books, 1988), p. 39.
  2. Einhard, *The Life of Charlemagne,* translated by Samuel Epes Turner, http://www.galileolibrary.com/ebooks/eu07/charlemagne_toc.htm, p. 4.
  3. John J. Butt, *Everyday Life in the Age of Charlemagne* (Westport, Connecticut: Greenwood Press, 2002), p. 5.

Chapter 2   Establishing a Reputation
  1. Einhard, *The Life of Charlemagne,* translated by Samuel Epes Turner, http://www.galileolibrary.com/ebooks/eu07/charlemagne_toc.htm, p. 7.
  2. Ibid., p. 10.

Chapter 3   Creating an Empire
  1. Friedrich Heer, *Charlemagne and His World* (New York: Macmillan Publishing Company, 1975), p. 128.

Chapter 4   The Carolingian Renaissance
  1. John J. Butt, *Everyday Life in the Age of Charlemagne* (Westport, Connecticut: Greenwood Press, 2002), p. 155.
  2. Einhard, *The Life of Charlemagne,* translated by Samuel Epes Turner, http://www.galileolibrary.com/ebooks/eu07/charlemagne_toc.htm, p. 28.
  3. Ibid., p. 20.

Chapter 5   The Emperor
  1. Bob Stewart, *Charlemagne: Founder of the Holy Roman Empire* (New York: Sterling Publishing Company, 1988), p. 39.
  2. Russell Chamberlin, *Charlemagne: Emperor of the Western World* (London, England: Grafton Books, 1986), p. 181.
  3. Ibid.
  4. Jacques Boussard, *The Civilization of Charlemagne,* translated by Frances Partridge (New York: McGraw-Hill Book Company, 1968), p. 217.

For Further Reading

For Young Adults

Banfield, Susan. *Charlemagne.* New York: Chelsea House Publishers, 1986.

Biel, Timothy Levi. *The Importance of Charlemagne.* San Diego: Lucent Books, 1997.

Greenblatt, Miriam. *Charlemagne and the Early Middle Ages.* Tarrytown, New York: Benchmark Books, 2002.

MacDonald, Fiona. *The World in the Time of Charlemagne.* Broomall, Pennsylvania: Chelsea House Publishers, 2002.

Sypeck, Jeff. *The Holy Roman Empire and Charlemagne in World History.* Berkeley Heights, New Jersey: Enslow Publishers, 2002.

Works Consulted

Becher, Matthias. *Charlemagne.* Translated by David S. Bachrach. New Haven, Connecticut: Yale University Press, 2003.

Boussard, Jacques. *The Civilization of Charlemagne.* Translated by Frances Partridge. New York: McGraw-Hill Book Company, 1968.

Butt, John J. *Daily Life in the Age of Charlemagne.* Westport, Connecticut: Greenwood Press, 2002.

Chamberlin, Russell. *Charlemagne: Emperor of the Western World.*

London, England: Grafton Books, 1986.

Einhard. *The Life of Charlemagne.* Translated by Samuel Epes Turner. Ann Arbor, Michigan: The University of Michigan Press, 1964; http://www.galileolibrary.com/ebooks/eu07/charlemagne_toc.htm

Heer, Friedrich. *Charlemagne and His World.* New York: Macmillan Publishing Company, 1975.

Hyslop, Stephen G. *Time Frame AD 600–800: The March of Islam.* Alexandria, Virginia: Time-Life Books, 1988.

Hyslop, Stephen G., and Brian Pohanka. *Time Frame AD 200–600: Empires Besieged.* Alexandria, Virginia: Time-Life Books, 1988.

Owen, D.D.R. *The Legend of Roland.* New York: Praeger Publishers, 1973.

Stewart, Bob. *Charlemagne: Founder of the Holy Roman Empire.* New York: Sterling Publishing Company, 1988.

On the Internet

Catholic Encyclopedia: "Charlemagne" http://www.newadvent.org/cathen/03610c.htm

The Carolingian Empire: "Charlemagne and His Heirs" http://www.royalty.nu/history/empires/Carolingian.html

For Further Reading

Charlemagne's the King
  http://www.chronique.com/Library/
  MedHistory/charlemagne.htm
The History Guide: "Charlemagne and the
  Carolingian Renaissance"
  http://www.historyguide.org/ancient/
  lecture20b.html

The Roman Empire, Part 7
  http://www.crystalinks.com/
  romanempire7.html
Schmandt, Raymond H. "The Holy
  Roman Empire."
  http://www.serendipity.li/twz/hre.html

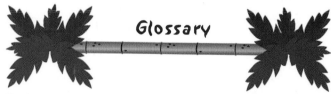

Glossary

abbot	(AH-but)—the head of a monastery.
barbarism	(BAR-buh-ri-zum)—acting with special cruelty; backward in thinking, or ignorant.
Carolingian	(kah-rah-LIN-jee-en)—having to do with the reign of Charles.
deposed	(dee-POZED)—removed from a high position of power.
freeman	(FREE-min)—a man with the full rights of a citizen; a man who isn't enslaved.
minstrels	(MIN-struls)—wandering musicians who recite poetry, usually accompanying themselves on small harps.
monastery	(MAH-nuh-stare-ee)—housing for men under religious vows; often includes gardens and fields where they raise food so that they can be self-sufficient.
pagans	(PAY-guns)—people who believe in several gods; people with little or no religious beliefs.
pious	(PYE-us)—showing deep religious beliefs.
Saracen	(SAH-rah-sen)—Having to do with the nomadic desert tribes originally from Arabia.
usurpation	(you-sur-PAY-shun)—seizing power without the right to do so.

Index